To: _____Doug_____

From: _____Mom_____

with much love

To A
Very Special
Son

Great Quotations Publishing Company

Compiled by Susanne Starck
Cover Design by Bostrom Publishing
Typeset and Design by Julie Otlewis

© 1996 Great Quotations Publishing Company

Published by Great Quotations Publishing Company
1967 Quincy Court
Glendale Heights, Illinois 60139

Printed in Hong Kong

ISBN: 1-56245-092-1

There are only two lasting bequests we can give our children. One of these is roots, the other, wings.

— Hodding Carter

A man is not old until regrets
take the place of dreams.

— John Barrymore

Humor brings insight
and tolerance.

— Agnes Repplier

When I was a small boy, my father told me never to recommend a church or a woman to anyone. And I have found it wise never to recommend a restaurant either. Something always goes wrong with the cheese souffle.

— Edmund G. Love

Laughter is the closest thing
to the grace of God.

— Karl Barth

You grow up the first time you
laugh - at yourself.

— Ethel Barrymore

The one serious conviction
that a man should have is
that nothing should be taken
too seriously.

— Nicholas Murray Butler

If you don't daydream and kind of plan things out in your imagination, you never get there.

— Robert Duvall

I was given incentive by my dad, who always says, "If you're going to do it, get it done."

— Charley Pride

Let us always meet each other
with a smile, for the smile is
the beginning of love.

— Mother Teresa

Do you know how parents spell relief? W-E-D-D-I-N-G! In case you haven't noticed, no one cries at weddings anymore.

— Erma Bombeck

Never work before breakfast;
if you have to work before
breakfast, eat your
breakfast first.

— Josh Billings

There is no more lovely, friendly, and charming relationship, communion, or company than a good marriage.

A man travels the world over
in search of what he needs and
returns home to find it.

— George Moore

You leave home to seek your fortune, and when you get it you go home and share it with your family.

— Anita Baker

My father said never look up to any other person and never look down to any person.

— Dorian Harewood

Big shots are only little shots
who keep shooting.

— Christopher Morley

The difficulties of life are
intended to make us better,
not bitter.

Even the woodpecker owes his success to the fact that he uses his head and keeps pecking away until he finishes the job he starts.

— Coleman Cox

We don't love a woman for what she says, we like what she says because we love her.

— Andre Naurois

My father gave me a trumpet because he loved my mother so much.

— Miles Davis

The safest way to double your
money is to fold it over once
and put it in your pocket.

— Frank McKinney Hubbard

A lot of fellows nowadays
have a B.A., M.D., or Ph.D.
Unfortunately, they don't
have a J.O.B..

— Fats Domino

It isn't the great big pleasures
that count the most;
it's making a great deal out of
the little ones.

— Jean Webster

Music is given to us specifically to make order of things, to move from an anarchic, individualistic state to a regulated, perfectly conscious one, which alone insures vitality and durability.

— Igor Stravinsky

When you reach for the stars,
you may not quite get one,
but you won't come up with a
handful of mud either.

— Leo Burnett

In three words I can sum up
everything I've learned
about life: It goes on.

— Robert Frost

Far and away the best prize
that life offers is the chance
to work hard at work
worth doing.

— Theodore Roosevelt

Never slap a man who
chews tobacco.

— Willard Scott

There are no wrong notes.

— Thelonius Monk

All you earnest young men
out to save the world -
please have a laugh.

— Reinhold Niebuhr

When you follow the path of
your father, you learn to walk
like him.

— Ashanti

There was never a good war
or a bad peace.

— Benjamin Franklin

Tell a female she's thin and
she's yours for life.

— Anne Bernays

It was my uncle who first taught me that cooking is neither a feminine nor a masculine category but is always a joyful and noisy event.

— Jeff Smith

There is only one success -
to be able to spend your life in
your own way.

— Christopher Morley

A good head and a
good heart are always a
formidable combination.

— Nelson Mandela

No one should negotiate their dreams. Dreams must be free to flee and fly high. No government, no legislature, has a right to limit your dreams. You should never agree to surrender your dreams.

— Jesse Jackson

Service is the rent that you
pay for room on this earth.

— Shirley Chisholm

If a young man tells me what
he aspires to be, I can almost
predict his future.

— Benjamin Mays

It isn't what you have in your
pocket that's important,
but what you have in
your heart.

— Cardinal Bernadin

Never say you don't know -
nod wisely, leave calmly, then
run like hell to find the
nearest expert.

— S. M. Oddo

The way to go from rags to riches is to start with a decent set of rags.

— Leonard Spinrad

There is a child in all of us, a person who believes in a glorious future.

— Jasmine Guy

How you handle defeat is not something to be taken lightly. You've got to think it through. Defeat is an art form, you've got to accept it, and you've got to move on. And once you do that, it's not bad.

— Walter Mondale

Do not use a hatchet to
remove a fly from your
friend's forehead.

— Chinese Proverb

Your children need your
presence more than
your presents.

— Jesse Jackson

I make money using my
brains and I lose money
listening to my heart. But in
the long run my books balance
pretty well.

— Kate Seredy

How lucky I was to have a father who, in spite of formidable obstacles, would fight for his beliefs and ambitions and win!

— Benjamin Davis, Jr.

My mother had a great deal
of trouble with me, but I think
she enjoyed it.

— Mark Twain

Never cut what you can untie.

— Joseph Joubert

You don't have to buy from
anyone. You don't have to
work at any particular job.
You don't have to participate
in any given relationship.
You can choose.

— Harry Browne

Make money your god and it
will plague you like the devil.

— Harry Fielding

Money is a good servant but
a bad master.

— Francis Bacon

No love, no friendship can cross the path of our destiny without leaving some mark on it forever.

— Francois Mauriac

Children make you want to
start life over.

— Muhammad Ali

Nothing grows well in the
shade of a big tree.

— Constantin

When you cease to make a
contribution you begin to die.

— Eleanor Roosevelt

Live together like brothers
and do business like strangers.

— Arab Proverb

He gets on best with women who have learned how to get on without him.

— Ambrose Bierce

Failure is a word that I simply don't accept.

—John H. Johnson

No matter how many
communes anybody invents
the family always creeps back.

— Margaret Mead

A child is the root of
the heart.

— Carolina Maria de Jesus

Dreamers have only one
owner at a time. That's why
dreamers are lonely.

— Erma Bombeck

What we play is life.

— Louis Armstrong

The only way to keep your health is to eat what you don't want, drink what you don't like, and do what you'd rather not.

— Mark Twain

I do not like broccoli.
And I haven't liked it since I
was a little kid and my mother
made me eat it. And I'm
President of the United States,
and I'm not going to eat any
more broccoli!

— George Bush

Only choose in marriage a woman you would choose as a friend if she were a man.

— Joseph Joubert

Make some muscles in your head but use the muscle in your heart.

— Ethiopian Proverb

The ache for home lives in all of us, the safe place where we can go as we are and not be questioned.

— Maya Angelou

The first principle is that you
must not fool yourself - and
you are the easiest person
to fool.

— Richard Feynman

Don't depend on a big
wheel to do you a good turn.

— Joan I. Welsh

Don't watch the clock -
do what it does. Keep going.

— Sam Levenson

Life is short, but truth works
far and lives long; let us speak
the truth.

— Arthur Schopenhauer

A journey of a thousand miles
must begin with a single step.

— Lao-tzu

All work is empty, save when there is love.

— Kahlil Gibran

You win some, you lose some, and some get rained out, but you gotta suit up for them all.

—J. Askenberg

Choose a job you love and you will never have to work a day in your life.

— Confucius

You can't base your life on other people's expectations.

— Stevie Wonder

There is something greater than wealth, grander even than fame. . . manhood and character, stand for success. . . nothing else really matters.

— Orison Swett Marden

The greatest thing in the world is to know how to belong to oneself.

— Montaigne

But what's more important. Building a bridge or taking care of a baby.

—June Jordan

The only way to get a
serious message across is
through comedy.

— Woody Harrelson

One generation plants the
trees; another gets the shade.

— Chinese Proverb

What I learned constructive about women is that no matter how old they get, always think of them the way they were on the best day they ever had.

— Ernest Hemingway

Your relationships with people begin in the home, where you learn values. It's the responsibility of the family.

— Melba Moore

It doesn't matter who my father was; it matters who I remembered he was.

— Anne Sexton

The child had every toy his father ever wanted.

— Robert E. Whitten

The sun will set without
thy assistance.

— The Talmud

A handful of patience is
worth more than a bushel
of brains.

— Dutch Proverb

Aim at the sun, and you may
not reach it; but your arrow
will fly higher than aimed
at an object on a level
with yourself.

— Joel Hawes

As a teenager, I rebelled and wanted to break out of the confines of my strict upbringing. But now I've mellowed and I'm becoming more like my father.

— Denzel Washington

When I was a boy of fourteen, my father was so ignorant I could hardly stand to have the old man around. But when I got to be 21, I was astonished to find how much he had learned in seven years.

— Mark Twain

There are things of deadly
earnest that can only be safely
mentioned under cover of
a joke.

—J. J. Procter

Music produces a kind of
pleasure which human nature
cannot do without.

— Confucious

When in doubt, look at what
the man who has the power
to hire or fire you, determine
your raise or promotion,
is wearing, and model
yourself on that. And if he's a
she, as may be the case,
look at the nearest male
authority figure you can find,
if there still is one.

— Michael Korda

Patience is a wonderful thing,
especially in a creditor.

You can't have everything.
Where would you put it?

— Steven Wright

We should gain more by letting ourselves be seen such as we are, than by attempting to appear what we are not.

— La Rochefoucauld

Hitch your wagon to a star.

— Ralph Waldo Emerson

Old men dream dreams;
young men see visions.

— Melvin B. Tolson

The best way to make your
dreams come true is to
wake up.

— Paul Valery

Rather than love, than
money, than fame,
give me truth.

— Thoreau

Humor is one of God's most marvelous gifts. Humor gives us smiles, laughter, and gaiety. Humor reveals the roses and hides the thorns. Humor makes our heavy burdens light and smooths the rough spots in our pathways. Humor endows us with the capacity to clarify the obscure, to simplify the complex, to deflate the pompous, to chastise the arrogant, to point a moral, and to adorn a tale.

— Sam Ervin

The pleasure of all reading is doubled when one lives with another who shares the same books.

— Katherine Mansfield

My father and I have the
same hands. We have the same
dreams. We write the same
lyrics, sometimes.

— Prince

Great men cultivate love . . .
only little men cherish the
spirit of hatred.

— Booker T. Washington

Always do right. This will
gratify some people and
astonish the rest.

— Mark Twain

You have to expect things
of yourself before you can
do them.

— Michael Jordan

Saving is a very fine thing,
especially when your parents
have done it for you.

— Winston Churchill

Talk about a dream.
Try to make it real.

— Bruce Springsteen

There is as much dignity is
tilling a field as in writing
a poem.

— Booker T. Washington

Happiness does not come
from what you have but from
what you are.

My pride keeps me going. That's why I work so hard . . . I was taught to play hard, though maybe I wasn't taught, I just watched my dad. I'm nothing more than my dad in the next generation. He always took time when I needed it for constructive criticism. He didn't holler at me like some fathers. He just tried to explain the right ways.

— Pete Rose

Some women are like Pompeii; some are like Verdun; some are like Kokomo, Indiana on a Sunday afternoon.

— Benjamin De Casseres

Music is your own experience, your thoughts, your wisdom. If you don't live it, it won't come out of your horn.

— Charlie Parker

Go out into the world, find work that you love, learn from your mistakes, and work hard to make a difference.

— Maurice R. Greenberg

None of us are responsible for our birth. Our responsibility is the use we make of our life.

— Joshua Henry Jones

Other Titles by Great Quotations Publishing Company
COMB BOUND

A Friend Is

A Smile Increases Your Face Value

Aged to Perfection

An Apple A Day

Backfield in Motion

Batter Up

Bedside Manner

Believe and Achieve

Best in Business Humor

Birthday Wishes

Books Are Better

Boyfriends Live Longer Than Husbands

Change Your Thoughts,
    Change Your Life

Don't Marry, Be Happy

Double Dribble

Golf Humor

Graduation - Keys To Success

Great Quotes - Great Comedians

Halfway Home (Surviving
    the Middle Years)

Harvest Of THoughts

Inspirations

Joy Of Family

Keys To Happiness

Life's Winning Tips

Love, Honor, Cherish

Love, Sex & Marriage

Love On Your Wedding Day

Mothers And Babies

Never Give Up

Our Life Together

Over The Hill Sex

Political Humor

Quotations from African-American

Real Friends

Retirement

Sports Poop

Sports Quotes

Stress

Teachers Inspirations

Thank You

The Quest For Success

Things You'll Learn

Thinking Of You

Thoughts From The Heart

To A Very Special Daughter

To A Very Special Son

To A Very Special Grandparent

To A Very Special Love

To My Mother

To My Father

Unofficial Christmas Survival Guide

Unofficial Executive Survival Guide

Unofficial Stress Test

Unofficial Survival Guide
    to Parenthood

Unofficial Vacation Guide

Ordinary Men, Extraordinary Lives

Our Thoughts Are Prayers

What To Tell Your Children

Who Really Said

Wonders & Joys Of Christmas

Words From Great Women

PAPERBACK

199 Useful Things to Do With
   A Politician
201 Best Things Ever Said
A Lifetime of Love
A Light Heart Lives Long
A Teacher Is Better Than Two Books
As A Cat Thinketh
Cheatnotes On Life
Chicken Soup
Dear Mr. President
Father Knows Best
Food For Thought
Golden Years/Golden Words
Happiness Walks On Busy Feet
Heal The World
Hooked on Golf
Hollywords
I'm Not Over The Hill

In Celebration of Women
Life's Simple Pleasures
Mother - A Bouquet of Love
Motivation Magic
Mrs. Webster's Dictionary
Reflections
Romantic Rendezvous
Sports Page
So Many Ways To Say
   Thank You
The ABC's of Parenting
The Best Of Friends
The Birthday Astrologer
The Little Book of
   Spiritual Wisdom
Things You'll Learn,
   If You Live Long Enough

PERPETUAL CALENDARS

Apple A Day
Country Proverbs
Each Day A New Beginning
Friends Forever
Golf Forever
Home Is Where The Heart Is
Proverbs
Seasonings
Simply The Best Dad
Simple The Best Mom
Simple Ways To Say I Love You
Teacher"s" Are "First Class!"

Great Quotations Publishing Company

1967 Quincy Court
Glendale Heights, IL 60139-2045
Phone (708) 582-2800
FAX (708) 582-2813